FOOTBALL

**All the skills you ever
wanted to learn**

Tim Edwards

Foreword by Harry Redknapp

p

This is a Parragon Book
This edition published in 2003

Parragon
Queen Street House
4 Queen Street
Bath, BA1 1HE, UK

Text ©Parragon
Photographs copyright ©EMPICS Ltd

Produced by Atlantic Publishing

A catalogue record for this book is available from the British Library.
ISBN 1 40541 533 9

Printed in China

CONTENTS

HARRY REDKNAPP

When Bobby Robson was asked what on earth he was doing still involved in the cauldron of top-level football in his late sixties, the answer he gave would have struck a chord with football fans everywhere. The Newcastle United boss said it was his work, his hobby, his life; and anyway, who wants to go shopping on a Saturday afternoon when there's a game on? Point taken.

Football unites us all. Whether you're a David Beckham, a minor league amateur or someone who just likes a kickabout in the park, the game remains the same: beautiful to behold and really quite simple.

The two big differences between the top players and the rest of us mere mortals are fitness and skill levels. We can all train hard, become faster and stronger. But what about skill? You've either got it or you haven't, right? Wrong!

Consider two of the greatest players of the modern era, George Best and Kevin Keegan. Best had amazing natural ability - that's true enough - but he still practised day after day on the streets of Belfast where he grew up. He would spend hours kicking a ball against gutters, garage doors, even doorknobs, learning how to control the awkward rebounds. And later he used this skill to brilliant effect on the biggest stages, cheekily playing one-twos off the shins of bewildered defenders!

Kevin Keegan's rise to the top is an even more dramatic example of the need for dedication and practice. He had nowhere near Best's natural ability and was told as a youngster that he would never make it. Keegan was utterly single-minded, however. He worked incredibly hard, making the most of what talent he had. Liverpool plucked him from lowly Scunthorpe, and he went on to captain England and become European Footballer of the Year. There's hope for us all!

So the message is clear: whether you're blessed with a lot of natural talent or not, you need to work hard on your game. And when you've perfected a skill, keep working on it until it becomes second nature. Why else do you think David Beckham stays behind after training to pepper the goal with his free-kick thunderbolts?

This book might not turn you into a Beckham, but it covers all the skills you'll need to become a good player, no matter what your position. There are top technique tips to improve your individual performance. There's also a detailed analysis of positional play, formations and tactics. This is an increasingly important part of football, for no matter how good you are on the ball, you have to remember that it is an 11-man game. Well-organized sides who attack and defend as a unit can often come out on top against a group of more talented individuals.

Whatever level you play at, or whether you're just a keen watcher, this book will help to improve your knowledge and understanding of the Beautiful Game.

Steven Gerrard goes through his warm-up routine.

Preparing for a game used to mean little more than a bit of passing and shooting practice while the captain tossed up in the centre circle. The influence of continental coaches such as Arsene Wenger and Gerard Houllier has helped to change our thinking about the way we prepare for a match or training session.

Warming-up

Before any strenuous activity, be it a training session or full-scale match, you should warm up thoroughly. Football is an explosive game. You might be standing still one second and going flat out the next. If your muscles aren't well stretched and loosened, you run the risk of straining them.

Stretching

Start with a gentle jog, gradually increasing your stride. Then do some side skips, using your arms to make a star shape. Now step it up to a side run, crossing the trailing leg in front of and behind the leading leg alternately. Work your way up to a flat-out sprint.

Stretching the quadriceps

To stretch the quadriceps adopt the positon shown, making sure you are well balanced. Repeat three times with each leg, holding the position for twenty seconds. Never 'bounce' or over stretch.

When you are warm, go through a stretching routine for all the major muscle groups. Obviously, the leg muscles will get most of the attention - that is, the hamstrings, calves, thighs and groin. Stretching the upper body muscles is essential for goalkeepers, but it is also a good idea for outfield players too. These muscles include the stomach, back, side, neck and shoulders.

Hamstring stretch

Sit on the floor and with your leg straight and then gradually move your outstretched hands towards your lower leg. Hold the position for twenty seconds.

Suppleness

For all stretching exercises, the movements should be gradual. Stretch into position and hold for twenty seconds, then release.

STRIKING THE BALL

David Beckham practises his shooting skills

The ball can be struck using a range of different techniques and a variety of contact surfaces. You don't have to be a master of all of them - many top professionals aren't - but the more technical weapons you have in your armoury, the more complete a player you will become.

Use both feet

One of the most common weaknesses is being one-footed. Many players use one leg to propel the ball and the other simply to stand on! Being two-footed has distinct advantages. First, if an opponent knows you will only deliver the ball with a particular foot, then you are removing one of the major uncertainty factors. Now, that may not always matter. There have been many internationals who have been almost exclusively one-footed. Knowing which foot a player is going to use to strike the ball and doing something about it are two completely different things. Nevertheless, if you are comfortable hitting the ball with either foot, you are preventing defenders from using one of their favourite tricks: pushing the player in possession on to his weaker foot.

The second advantage of being two-footed is that it can buy time and space. If you receive the ball on your weaker side, you will inevitably lose valuable time in transferring it to your stronger foot - possibly enough time for a defender to get in a challenge.

Finally, it should be noted that most ball-striking techniques are used for both passing and shooting. Both involve delivering the ball with a target in mind: with passing, the target is a team-mate; with shooting, it is the back of the net.

Practise striking the ball with both feet. If you are comfortable hitting the ball off both sides, you can prevent defenders from using one of their favourite tricks: pushing the player in possession on to his weaker foot.

THE PUSH PASS

The basic side-foot pass, or push pass, is the bread-and-butter method of delivering the ball for all teams. The ball is stroked along the ground using the large surface area of the side of the boot. It is the most accurate and reliable way of striking the ball, but the amount of power generated is limited, so it is only useful over short distances. The pass-and-move approach to the game is all about accurate short passing; in effect, it could be said that the tactics of the modern era are underpinned by the push pass. In spite of its name, the push pass is often used by goal poachers to stroke the ball into the net.

- The non-kicking foot should be placed alongside the ball
- Head and body should be over the ball at the point of contact
- Strike through the midline of the ball. The striking foot should be at right angles to the direction of the pass
- Always follow through

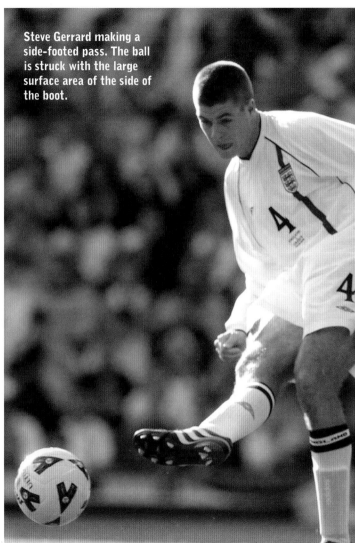

Steve Gerrard making a side-footed pass. The ball is struck with the large surface area of the side of the boot.

DRIVING THE BALL

Despite the importance of the short passing game, it does have the disadvantage of being a slower, more methodical build-up. The more direct approach afforded by the longer ball can take several defenders out of the game at a stroke. David Beckham and Steven Gerrard are two of the best exponents of the long, raking pass. The side-foot technique is no use for hitting 50-yard passes; instead, the ball is driven with the instep.

There are two variations on the drive, depending on whether you want to keep the ball low or loft it through the air. The former is better suited to shooting, the latter comes into its own in long passing.

- **For the low drive,** the approach should be at a slight angle. The non-kicking foot is placed close to the ball

- **With toes pointing down,** strike through the centre of the ball

- **For the lofted drive,** approach from a slightly wider angle. Place the non-kicking foot a little behind the ball. Strike through the centre of the ball, but this time below the horizontal midline

- **When driving the ball,** most young players make the mistake of trying to hit the leather off it. Timing and technique are far more important. David Beckham regularly hits 50-yard passes and makes it look quite effortless

The low drive
The non-kicking foot is placed close to the ball.
With toes pointing down, strike through the centre of the ball.

At one time, bending the ball was seen as a very innovative technique, the preserve of Brazilian maestros. These days, it is an extremely common skill. It is certainly not a party piece. Swerving passes can be used to take opponents out of the game, find team-mates who couldn't be reached with another kind of pass, and exploit space. Swerving shots can be used to bend the ball round a keeper's outstretched hand and into the net.

Sidespin

To swerve the ball you must strike it off-centre. Striking the ball just off-centre will give more power and less spin; a more glancing contact will give more spin and less power. Similarly, striking the ball through the horizontal midline will keep the ball low; striking below the horizontal midline will make it rise. All these various permutations are easier to practise than to describe! If you experiment with striking the ball in all these different ways, you will soon begin to develop a feel for what kind of contact brings about a particular result.

SWERVING THE BALL

- **Practise swerving the ball** with the inside of the foot first
- **The kicking foot** strikes across the ball from inside to outside (ie from left to right if you are right-footed, and vice versa). Contact should be made around the base of the big toe
- **On making contact,** rotate the foot. This is often described as "wrapping the foot around the ball". It is the technique that David Beckham uses to such devastating effect in his long passing and from dead-ball situations
- **To swerve the ball** with the outside of the foot, place the non-kicking foot a little behind and to the side of the ball
- **The kicking foot** comes across the body from outside to inside (ie for a right-footed player the boot comes across the body to strike the left-hand side of ball, and vice versa). Toes should be pointing down at moment of contact
- **With all swerving passes** the follow-through is very important

To swerve the ball you must strike it off-centre.

THE VOLLEY

The big advantage of the volley – striking the ball first time instead of controlling it – is speed. Defenders have little time to react, and if you are shooting, goalkeepers might be taken by surprise.

It isn't easy to strike a ball that might be coming towards you, going across you, or dropping out of the air. The key is to get your body into a good position early and not to abandon good technique in favour of a wild swing! It's timing that is required, not brute force.

Volleys can be defined in two ways: one is the part of the foot that is used to strike the ball, the other is where the ball is in relation to the body.

Side-foot or instep?

The side-foot and instep can both be used to volley the ball. The difference between the two is very similar to the difference between the push pass and the drive. In other words, the side-foot volley - just like the side-foot pass - offers greater accuracy and reliability but less power. An instep volley - just like an instep drive - generates a lot of power, but the contact surface is much smaller so there is a greater margin for error.

Generally speaking, the side-foot volley is used for an instant lay-off to a team-mate. If the ball is arriving at pace, the volleyer can cushion the ball as he guides it towards the receiver. The instep volley is often used by defenders clearing their lines or strikers shooting for goal.

Strike the ball centrally with the toes pointing downwards. Make sure your body is over the ball.

Side volley

The body rotates around the standing leg as you strike the ball. Timing and body shape must be perfect.

2. Volleying from the side

This will nearly always be an instep volley. It is most commonly associated with shooting, though it can be used as a passing technique. The body rotates around the standing leg as you strike the ball. As the kicking foot comes across the body, there will be a natural tendency to fall away. This won't matter after you have gone through with the shot, but any loss of balance as you are shaping to shoot will almost certainly result in a poor delivery. Ideally, contact should be made through the centre of the ball. Sometimes, players err on the side of caution and get over the ball, driving it into the ground. Although this will take some pace off the shot, it is no bad technique to use since goalkeepers dislike balls bouncing in front of them.

1. Volleying from the front

Either the side-foot or instep technique can be used from this position. If a power volley is required, strike the ball centrally with the toes pointing downwards. Make sure your body is over the ball. If you are leaning backwards, you won't be able to keep the ball down. That won't matter for a defender making a clearance, but for a striker going for goal it will almost inevitably mean the ball sailing over the bar.

The side-foot volley pass is really a midair version of the push pass. You must be well balanced on your standing leg. Guide the ball to the receiver with the foot at right angles to the direction of the pass.

3. Overhead Kick

If you were grading the various football skills by their degree of difficulty, the overhead kick definitely would come into the "advanced" category. The margin of error with this acrobatic technique is extremely small. If your timing is even fractionally out, the ball can finish up well off target - and you may not make contact at all! Don't worry; even the pros can't manage a high success rate with this technique.

Confidence

Because the overhead kick requires perfect timing and touch, it really helps if a player is in good form and very confident. Having said all that, if the ball is in the air and you have your back to goal, the overhead kick can be just the thing to take an unwary goalkeeper by surprise. Of course, you could lay the ball off to a team-mate, or maybe control the ball and turn. Indeed, you will probably take one of those options most of the time. But occasionally, an overhead kick is well worth the risk. Like all snap shots, it has the advantage of cutting down the reaction time of both the defenders and the goalkeeper.

Strike with the instep

Take off with your kicking leg. Raise your non-kicking leg and lean back. Use your arms to maintain good balance, and keep your eye on the ball. Bring your kicking leg through and strike the ball with the instep. The leg should be outstretched, with toes curled forward so that you can get over the ball. This is particularly important if you are striking for goal, less so if you are in defence and merely trying to clear your lines. As the kicking leg whips through the ball, the non-striking leg naturally drops to act as a counterbalance. The way the two legs cross has given this technique its other common name, the "scissor kick".Be very careful when practising overhead kicks. Your non-kicking foot and hands should hit the ground first to break your fall. In particular, avoid letting your back, shoulders or neck take the full impact. The potential for injury is obviously greater on hard ground. For that reason, practise this skill on a soft surface, perhaps even using mats.

Overhead kick

Your non-kicking foot and hands should hit the ground first to break your fall. In particular, avoid letting your back, shoulders or neck take the full impact.

Zoltan Sebescen stabs under the ball for the perfect chip.

THE CHIP

Hitting the ball up in the air isn't too difficult. Getting it up, over opponents and down again into a tight space (ball into the net!) is a little more tricky. This is when the chip comes into its own.

To chip the ball the non-kicking foot should be close to the ball. The kicking foot stabs down under the ball but does not follow through. The ball rises steeply; it is possible to get it over the head of opponents standing just a few yards away. The stabbing action puts backspin on the ball, making it hold up sharply as it pitches on the turf. This makes it a very effective weapon against a defence which is pushing up. If you can drop the ball beyond the last defender, and a team-mate can time his run to beat the offside trap, a goalscoring opportunity could be created. The chip is equally important as a means of beating an advancing goalkeeper in a one-on-one situation.

The Chip

The non-kicking foot should be close to the ball. The kicking foot stabs down under the ball but does not follow through.

PASSING

Thorsten
Fink

Football is a team game. It is all about blending diverse talents into a tight, effective unit. A team that operates well collectively will perform at a much higher level than the skills of the individual players might suggest. To play as a unit, teams must be adept at passing the ball.

Passing and movement

Virtuoso individual performances can win games, but they can't be used as the basis for a team's tactics, or a guide to a team's form. The first and foremost consideration of any top coach analysing a game is the quality of the passing and movement.

We have already looked at the techniques used for passing the ball. But passing is a skill, not just a technique. It isn't enough simply to learn how to strike the ball well. Let's look at some of the wider aspects of good passing.

Pass selection

The player in possession ought to have a range of passing options open to him. Good support play will ensure this is so. The player on the ball must then decide which team-mate to pass to. Every decision will have a risk/reward factor. A long through-ball, especially on the ground, is very risky but might be worth it if a goalscoring opportunity can be created. On the other hand, a 10-yard sideways or backwards pass might be risk-free, but neither does it pose any threat to the opposition. That isn't to say that the "negative" pass is always wrong. Indeed, moving the ball around in this way while looking for a good attacking opening might be the very thing to do.

To make pass selection as easy as possible, players must learn to play with their heads up. Your awareness of what is happening around you will be severely restricted if you spend too much time looking at the ball.

If weighing up the value of each pass isn't difficult enough, the picture can change totally in a second. This leads to the next consideration: timing.

Play with your head up

To make pass selection as easy as possible, players must learn to play with their heads up. Your awareness of what is happening around you will be severely restricted if you spend too much time looking at the ball.

SUCCESSFUL PASSING

1. Timing

Football is a fast and furious game. An excellent choice of pass one moment could be a poor option if made a fraction too soon or too late. The receiver has to share some responsibility in this regard. Well-timed passing requires both passer and receiver to be on the same wavelength. They may use little signals as a means of agreeing when and where the pass will be delivered.

2. Direction, height and pace

The decision to pass to a particular team-mate prompts several more decisions that have to be made. Are you going to play the ball in the air or along the deck? Will you play the ball to his feet or into space? How much pace will you put on the ball? Let's examine each in turn.

When judging what height of pass to make, remember that the ground pass is direct and will get to the receiver more quickly. It will also be easier for him to control. The downside to such passes is the risk of interception, particularly when played over distance.

As a general rule, in tighter situations you should play the ball to feet. In a congested midfield area, for example, there won't be much space and a ball played even a couple of yards wide of the receiver could result in loss of possession. Down the flanks and behind the defenders it could be a very different picture. If a player has space in front of him to move into, then the ball could be played several yards ahead of the receiver without risk.

3. Weighting the pass

Once you have got the height and direction right, you now have to get the correct weight on the ball. Too much pace will make it hard to control when played to feet.

Accurate passing is the key skill in football. It is the means by which individual team members combine for a common purpose. A good pass employs three fundamental skills; selection, timing and execution.

Passing is the most practised aspect of football at every standard throughout the game. Seen here are players from the England team going through their passing drills in training.

4. Disguise

Finally, a pass which meets all the other quality criteria will be unsuccessful if the player makes his intentions obvious. "Telegraphing" a pass gives a signal to the opposition as well as your team-mates. A whole range of feints and dummies can also be used to disguise a pass. Watch the top players in action and perhaps develop a few tricks of your own! Remember, adding disguise to your passing isn't just a neat trick. Such passes will give the receiver more time on the ball, time that he may use to your team's advantage and the opposition's misfortune.

To sum up

Passing is the key skill in football. It is the means by which individual team members combine for a common purpose: defending one goal and attacking the other. Passing shouldn't be seen in isolation. Good movement is the opposite side of the coin. Young players often make the mistake of making such a good pass that they can't resist stopping to admire it! Good players are on the move as soon as the pass is delivered, looking to support the man in possession and make sure he has plenty of options. Coaches might enthuse over flashes of individual brilliance – a mazy dribble or overhead kick, for example – but these are the icing on the cake. Passing and moving are the lifeblood of every successful team.

Herbert Wieger (front)
and Julio Suazo.

Football is a passing game. On average, four out of five times when a player is in possession he will pass the ball. That is only half the story, of course. For every pass that is delivered, another player has to receive it. Ball control can thus be considered as 50 per cent of the passing game.

Creating time and space

A player may sometimes have the luxury of controlling a perfectly weighted and directed pass while in plenty of space. More often he will have to deal with a ball that might be bouncing or spinning awkwardly and with an opponent snapping at his heels. Instant control under pressure is the hallmark of a class player. It is a fine skill to behold and on occasions it can almost be worthy of applause in its own right. Go ahead and applaud if you wish, but you may be in danger of missing the point. Wonderful one-touch control achieves nothing in itself. What it does is give the player valuable extra time on the ball. This has two important advantages. First, it reduces the possibility of a defender getting in a challenge. This is because a player is at his most vulnerable when he is receiving the ball. Instant control thus makes the window of opportunity for the defender as small as possible. Second, good control allows a player to initiate his next move more quickly. Whether he decides to pass himself, run with the ball, dribble or shoot, he will be in a position to do so that little bit sooner.

Anticipation

The first element of good control is anticipation. Remember that we are not only talking about receiving a deliberate pass from a team-mate. There are also clearances from goalkeepers and defenders, deflections and stray passes from opponents. Anticipating where the ball is heading and getting into line as early as possible are big steps along the way to controlling it.

Side of the foot

This is the most used and most effective way of bringing the ball under control. Watch the ball on to the side of your foot then pull the foot back on impact to cushion the ball to the ground in front of you. Practise against a wall, varying the pace and height of the ball as it returns to you.

Controlling the ball

Now you have to decide whether you are going to cushion the ball or use your controlling touch to play it in a particular direction. Generally, in a congested area, cushion control will be needed. This means taking the pace out of the ball by relaxing the contact surface. But killing the ball at your feet is by no means always appropriate. If you are a striker, having the ball stuck between your feet is extremely awkward. Professionals talk about needing an extra touch to "get the ball out of your feet". That extra touch takes time, and a chance might go begging.

In any area of the pitch you should use your first touch to guide the ball in a particular direction, as long as space allows. This could be to set up a dribble or shooting opportunity; it could be simply to shield the ball from an opponent.

Guiding the ball

One of the best examples of using first touch to guide the ball instead of killing it came in the famous England versus Argentina match in the 1998 World Cup. From a deep position, David Beckham played the ball up to Michael Owen, who was near the halfway line. Owen saw that he had space in front of him, so he helped the ball on with the outside of his right boot. A few touches and a few seconds later, the ball was in the back of Argentina's net. Had Owen killed the ball with his first touch he might well have been closed down by a defender and forced to lay it off, and we wouldn't have witnessed one of the best World Cup goals ever scored.

To sum up, good control - and particularly good first touch - is a key skill.

It buys time and space, the most important commodities on the football field. And the more time and space a player has, the more likely he is to make his use of the ball count.

Thigh trap

Get into line with the flight of the ball. Bring your thigh up and on impact, drop it down. Aim to make contact with the ball as high up the thigh as possible. By introducing an element of resistance the ball can be set up for a volley. Conversely, by relaxing the thigh the ball can be dropped at your feet.

Sole of the foot

Contact is made as the ball hits the ground as the ball is wedged under the foot to stop it bouncing away. Watch the ball carefully. Split second timing is crucial to stop the ball running away from you.

Chest trap

The chest is a large area on which to catch the ball so there is a good margin of error. It is particularly important to make sure you have read the line of flight because it will be hard to change position after you have set your body to receive the ball. You can either decide to cushion the ball or use your controlling touch to play it in a particular direction.

1. Firm control

If the ball is travelling very fast there is often no option other than to keep the body solid on impact and guide it down to the ground. Here it is important to get well on top of the ball.

2. Cushion control

The key point to bear in mind with cushion control is that the part of the body receiving the ball must yield on impact. A rigid, tense surface will cause the ball to rebound away from the body. Practise relaxing the muscles and withdrawing the foot (or thigh or chest) at the point of contact so as to take the pace off the ball.

SHOOTING

Czech Republic's
Vladimir Smicer.

When your team is in possession, the name of the game is to create as many chances as possible, and put as many of those chances away as you can. Attractive build-up play is all very well, but it's goals that count. And the single most important thing a team can do to maximise its scoring potential is to get as many shots on target as it can. If this sounds obvious, then it is surprising how many teams disregard this advice.

With the responsibility of shooting comes a fear of failure. The ball might hit the corner flag and you might be criticised for not passing to a well-positioned team-mate. This is entirely the wrong attitude. Even the Robbie Fowlers of this world occasionally balloon a shot well over the bar, but that doesn't stop them eagerly awaiting their next shooting opportunity. Unless a player shoots from an impossible distance or angle, he should be encouraged rather than blamed.

Shoot first

So the advice is simple. Make shooting your first thought, and only if the shot isn't on should you consider other options.

Shooting is partly instinctive. Top strikers seem to have an uncanny knack for knowing where the goal is, even if they have their back to the target. Having said that, there are techniques that can be practised and tips that can be followed to improve a player's shooting.

Constant practice

Constant practice allows you to shoot with good technique even under pressure.

SHOOTING SKILLS

1. Aim low

Goalkeepers prefer rising shots; it is much easier for them to spring up for a high ball than to get down to a low shot. Also, a low shot might be deflected. And even if it is well off target it might fall invitingly at the feet of a team-mate and turn into an astute pass!

2. Shoot early

Players with poor technique or who are out of form and lacking in confidence often take an extra second and an extra touch to set themselves up for a shot. Dwelling on the ball in this way can result in a lost opportunity. Snap shots pay dividends. They allow defenders less time to get in a challenge, and goalkeepers less time to position themselves.

3. Accuracy or power?

If you imagine the 6-yard box extended to the penalty spot, that forms a rectangle inside which the vast majority of goals are scored. From such a close range, accuracy is more important than power. Much better to pass the ball into the corner of the net than to try a hopeful blast aimed at the centre of the goal. That shouldn't undermine the importance of distance shooting, however.

A 25-yard effort might have an element of surprise, and if there is a crowded box, the keeper's view might be obscured. The Brazilians have recognised the value of long-range shooting for many years, with Real Madrid's Roberto Carlos their current thunderbolt specialist. Scoring from distance has helped Brazil to lift the World Cup on a record four occasions. In practice, all shots are a combination of accuracy and power.

Even the hardest-struck efforts on goal ought to have a measure of control about them.

Lorenzo Amoruso shoots with power.

HEADING

Christian Correia Dionisio rises to head the ball.

There are two big obstacles to overcome when it comes to heading the ball. The first is fear. When a ball is hurtling towards your face, the natural reaction is to treat it like any other missile. Self-preservation takes over and we want to shield ourselves, duck, turn our head away and close our eyes. To be good in the air, players must learn to suppress these reactions. Once the fear factor has been overcome, the second hurdle is to master an extremely complex skill. The timing has to be absolutely perfect to meet the ball and send it in the required direction. Doing so while under the pressure of a challenge makes this doubly difficult.

Aerial power

Football purists don't like to see too many high balls and aerial battles. They maintain that the game is meant to be played on the ground, with ball to feet. While there is a lot of truth in this, aerial power has always been an important feature of the British game. Superb headers of the ball such as Teddy Sheringham and Alan Shearer are following in a long tradition of expertise in this aspect of the game. Also, it should be remembered that even the best defenders can't do much about a ball sailing over their heads. The combination of good aerial passes and powerful headers of the ball can be an excellent attacking ploy. Indeed, something like one goal in five is scored from a header. No team can afford to ignore an attacking weapon of such potential.

Attacking the ball

Let's look at the basic technique for heading the ball, then how it can be applied in different ways to perform different kinds of header.

Meet the ball with the forehead. There are three reasons for this. The skull is at its thickest here, and even a ball travelling at pace won't hurt; the surface is relatively flat, making controlling the direction of header that much easier; and meeting the ball just above eye level will help a player to watch it right up to the point of impact.

Strike the ball, don't let it strike you. It is important to attack the ball with confidence. Holding back and waiting for the ball to arrive is to invite an interception.

Use the back and neck muscles in tandem to generate forward momentum. By punching through the ball using the neck muscles, you will impart maximum power on to the ball. One exception in this regard is the cushioned header, which is discussed later.

DIFFERENT TYPES OF HEADER

1. Defensive header

The priority here is to clear the danger zone, so it is vital to get maximum height, width and distance. You may be giving away possession, but the theory is that if the ball is headed well outside the defensive third, then your team will have the opportunity to get in a good position to win it back in a less dangerous area. Contact with the ball should be made just below the horizontal midline. You certainly don't want to get over the ball and head it downwards, possibly to a striker's feet. And if you get underneath it too much, you will send the ball high into the air but won't get much distance.

If you are deep inside your own area or facing your own goal, then heading the ball out of play for a corner or throw-in might be a better option. Finally, remember that heading the ball back to your goalkeeper does not constitute a backpass. However, great care should be taken, particularly if speedy strikers are on hand to latch on to any underhit ball. If possible, headed backpasses should be cushioned and wide of goal, just to be on the safe side. Cushioned headers will be dealt with separately.

Practise first

Heading skills should be developed slowly. To begin with, practise getting your timing right with a static ball, perhaps suspended from the crossbar. You can then move on to attacking a moving ball thrown by a partner. The acid test will come in a game situation, when you will have to compete for the ball against real opponents.

Defensive header

It is vital to get maximum height, width and distance. Contact with the ball should be made just below the horizontal midline.

Attacking header

❶ Timing of the run and jump is important.

❷ Contact with the ball should be above the horizontal midline. Get well over the ball to head it down. Arch your back and snap forward at the point of impact.

2. Attacking header

Accuracy is obviously far more important here. With a goal measuring just eight yards by eight feet, the attacker has a much smaller target area than a defender clearing his lines. And with a goalkeeper to beat, the attacker can't afford to sacrifice too much power either. The attacker's first priority must be to get ahead of the defender and get to the ball first. The timing of the run, and also the jump if required, must be spot on.

If you are in a fairly central position relative to the goal, you have the choice of directing your header towards the near or far post. If you are at the far post, you will be powering the ball back the way it has come, either trying to beat the keeper at his near post or heading the ball back across the face of goal towards the far post.

3. Glancing header

If you are in front of the near post, or if the ball is played into the box from a deep position, then a glancing header will be needed. Here, you are using the forehead to redirect the ball. A fuller contact will be required if you are aiming for the near post, a more delicate contact if you're going for the far post. You can't generate much power with a glancing header; most of the pace on the ball comes from the delivery. Judging the angle of deflection off the forehead is not easy. Only experience and practice will help you develop a feel for the kind of contact required.

4. The flick on

A variation of the glancing header is the flick on. Here, the attacker allows the ball to skim off the forehead or top of the head. Many teams use this tactic at corner kicks. One attacker flicks the ball on at the near post, while his team-mates time their runs to arrive at the far post area. Defenders can be caught out by the change of direction on the ball, whereas the attacking side has the advantage of being able to anticipate such a delivery.

Finally, remember that when you go for goal with a header, a low ball will cause most problems for the goalkeeper. To direct the ball downwards you must get over it, making contact above the horizontal midline.

5. Cushioned header

If you are using a header to pass to a team-mate or back to the goalkeeper, the normal rules for all passing still apply. That means putting the ball in an area and at a pace that will help the receiver to control the ball comfortably. He certainly won't

thank you for a bullet header coming straight at him from five yards! This is when the cushioned header comes into its own. Just as you withdraw your foot to take the pace off a ball played along the ground, so you allow your head to "give" for a ball played in the air. By relaxing your neck and back muscles, your forehead absorbs power instead of generating it, and the result should be a nicely weighted pass for your team-mate.

A cushioned header can be just as effective in attack. If a cross has come in to the penalty area with too much pace because the winger was under pressure the same technique can be used to loop the ball into the net rather than power it over the bar.

It is important to attack the ball with confidence. Holding back and waiting for the ball to arrive is to invite an interception.

Jeff Kenna using his forehead to redirect the ball. A fuller contact will be required if you are aiming for the near post, a more delicate contact if you're going for the far post. For a strong deflection, twist the body with the head. This will mean you end up facing the direction in which you want the ball to go.

TURNING AND DRIBBLING

Holland's
Patrick Paauwe (r)
and England's
Emile Heskey.

There is no better sight in football than a player with the ball seemingly tied to his feet, taking on defender after defender and leaving them beaten and bewildered. In a tight game involving two well-drilled defences, players might struggle to find the time and space necessary to create goalscoring opportunities. In these kind of games the dribbling artists can really come into their own.

Creating space

Once a player goes past an opponent, he opens up space for himself. Another defender will be forced to come and challenge, even if that means leaving the player he is marking. In short, the whole defence can quickly unravel if a clever dribbler can take one or two players out of the game.

Mesmerising dribble

One of the best goals ever scored came after a mesmerising dribble from the great Diego Maradona. It happened in the quarter-finals of the 1986 World Cup, when England came up against Argentina. Maradona scored both goals in Argentina's victory. He punched the ball into the net for the first, but the second goal was pure magic. He ran half of the length of the pitch and beat half the England team before slotting the ball into the net. Twelve years later, at France 98, the two teams met again. This time it was Michael Owen who scored a wonder goal. Owen picked up the ball in a similar position to Maradona but he evaded the defenders more through blistering pace than marvellous footwork. Young players tend to watch the tricks that

players like Maradona and Owen use to beat defenders. However, most go on to develop their own style. With dribbling techniques, there are no hard and fast rules. If it works, use it. Having said that, although players such as Craig Bellamy, Michael Owen and Ryan Giggs might appear very different in style, they all use variations on the same basic ideas. Let's look at some of them.

DRIBBLING

Good close control is vital

Ideally, the ball should remain within playing distance at all times. There will be exceptions, of course. If a lot of space has opened up in front of you, or if sheer pace is your main weapon, then playing the ball further away from your body might be appropriate.

Not all good dribblers are speed merchants

In fact, change of gear can be just as effective as out-and-out pace. A player like Paul Gascoigne regularly beats players with excellent close control and quick bursts of acceleration over 10 or 15 yards.

Changes of direction can be just as disconcerting for defenders as changes of pace

By twisting and turning, the attacker will force the defender into adjusting his stride pattern and body position. Ryan Giggs does this probably better than anybody. Defenders are frequently left back-pedalling and off balance, sometimes struggling to stay on their feet, never mind make a tackle!

Vary which part of the boot makes contact with the ball

The inside and outside of both feet give four basic contact surfaces. Dragbacks using the soles of the feet give two more. The more variety you have in your dribbling technique, the more unsettling it will be for defenders.

Use feints and dummies

There are any number of ways to introduce these into your dribbling technique. One of the most basic is to step over or arc around the ball with one foot, then play it in the opposite direction with the other. Emile Heskey and Steve McManaman both favour this trick. It is surprising that even when a defender knows what might be coming, it still works nearly every time if well executed.

Protect the ball

If you keep your body between the ball and the chasing defender, he will find it difficult to tackle cleanly.

Play with your head up

You should keep your eye on the ball when you're playing it, but between touches you should glance up and be aware of how the play is developing around you. Even top players can be at fault in this regard. David Ginola is a masterful dribbler, but has often been criticised for the lack of end product to his work. Beating three players only to be dispossessed by the fourth may be highly entertaining but it is of little value to the team.

Don't be afraid of failure

Providing you are not deep inside your own territory - where the risks outweigh the benefits - take your opponent on with confidence. As with shooting, after several unsuccessful attempts you might hit the jackpot with the next. A player deserves more applause for trying to beat his man than for taking the soft option of a negative pass.

Dropping the shoulder

❶ Here the attacking player runs towards the defender, transferring his body weight to his left so that it looks as if he is going to move in that direction. An exaggerated drop of the shoulder helps to convince the defender of his intentions.

❷ The defender moves to intercept and has already begun to commit himself when the attacker changes direction. With the defender's body weight on his right leg, the attacking player accelerates past him on the opposite side.

Alessandro Del `Piero during training. Develop your ability to turn quickly by running slalom style through posts or any markers. This will also build up your quadriceps and improve your speed over short distances.

Good technique

In summary, although the emphasis in the modern game is on passing and moving, dribbling skills can open up the tightest defences. All players should work on their technique; dribbling isn't just for flying wingers.

Finally, it ought to be said that even unsuccessful dribbles can reap rewards. That is because dribbling often results in a set play. Good tackles frequently knock the ball out for a throw-in or corner; foul tackles lead to direct free kicks or penalties. As so many goals come from set pieces, it can be said that dribbling contributes both directly and indirectly towards creating scoring opportunities.

The step-over

❶ ❷   The attacker makes as if to play the ball with the outside of his left foot.

❸   Instead, he swings his foot over the ball and plants it on the ground.

❹   He pushes off this foot and goes past his opponent on the right, playing the ball with his right foot as he does so.

TURNING

Before you can dribble you have to make space for yourself. Often you will have your back to a defender which means you either have to play the ball back to a team-mate or turn and beat your marker.

If you are near your own goal you should show greater caution and play the way you are facing. However, in the attacking third, there are advantages to turning and trying to go past your marker. If you pass him you can take him out of the game, but even if you only make some space for yourself a shooting opportunity can arise.

Turning while closely marked

1. Keep your body between your opponent and the ball and use your body strength against the defender as he pushes into you. Good balance is essential.

2. You can screen the ball to block any attempt by your opponent to get round you. Keep the ball close to you. When the player is right up against your back this could be the opportunity to turn against him. This needs to be timed perfectly. You must turn just at the time he tries to come around your side to make a challenge.

If the ball is well away from your body, beyond your playing distance, blocking an opponent in this way would be deemed obstruction and result in a free kick. You can only shield the ball when it is in your possession.

Marcel Rath (front) and Pal Dardai. When the defender is tight against you this could be the opportunity to spin off him and accelerate away.

TACKLING AND DEFENDING

Borussia Monchengladbach's Marcin Mieciel (l)
slide tackles Bayern Munich's Michael Tarnat (r)

If the opposition has the ball, you can gain possession in one of two ways. One is the direct method, the tackle. The other way is by taking up good defensive positions, denying time and space, pressurising the man on the ball and forcing a mistake. Tackling is thus just one aspect of the defender's art. Let's look at tackling techniques, and then at the broader subject of defending.

The golden rule

The golden rule is to tackle when you are sure of winning the ball; otherwise, jockey the attacker and bide your time.

There are exceptions, of course. A striker in an advanced position might take a chance with a tackle, knowing that there is potentially a rich reward if it is successful, and little risk if he fails to win the ball. Also, a defender can't back off and jockey indefinitely! If he's retreating into his box, or an attacker is through on goal, then a defender might have to commit to a tackle whatever the circumstances.

Timing

A player is at his most vulnerable when he is receiving the ball, and this is the best time to make a tackle. Once he has it under control, take a more cautious approach. Keep your eye on the ball, not on any fancy footwork or body feints. On the other hand, if you feint to tackle, it might force a mistake from the attacker. Wait for the moment that the ball is beyond his playing distance, then make your move.

Once you have decided to commit to a tackle, the key factors are speed, determination, accuracy and timing. All of these are necessary if you are going to win the ball cleanly and not commit a foul.

TACKLING

Whoever gets more foot on the ball and drives through the challenge with their body weight is likely to win the ball.

Block tackle

The block tackle is the most common challenge in football, and can be made from the front or side. In the front-on tackle, you should place your standing foot beside the ball and drive through the challenge with your body weight behind the tackling leg. Contact is made with the side of the foot through the middle of the ball.

The side-on block tackle occurs when the attacker and defender are side-by-side rather than facing each other. The tackler gets as close as possible, then pivots on his standing leg, bringing the tackling foot round to make contact with the ball, using the same side-foot technique.

Although only the foot makes contact with the ball, the whole body makes the tackle. Approach the tackle as if making a side-foot pass and meet the ball solidly with the side of the foot. A low, well-balanced body will give the most chance of success.

Here, player ❶ has more foot in contact with the ball because he is using the side of his foot and is therefore likely to win the challenge. Player ❷ is attempting to win the ball with the power of his instep, where there is less surface area in contact with the ball. Timing is important. Be committed to the tackle. It only hurts if you pull out of it at the last moment.

Slide tackle

The slide tackle is a challenge of total commitment, since you are out of the game for a few precious moments if you don't win the ball. In fact, the basic rule is to stay on your feet whenever possible. However, slide tackles do allow defenders to make up valuable extra ground, and perhaps enable a player to reach the ball earlier than if he took an extra stride. If a defender is chasing a player who is through on goal, that fraction of a second gained by making a slide tackle could be the difference between getting in a challenge or not.

Most slide tackles are made from the side or from behind. In the latter case in particular, the tackler must ensure he makes contact with the ball first, not the attacker's leg, or he will concede a free kick. Ideally, the tackle should be made with the leg furthest away from the ball. In practice, many players tackle with their strongest leg, no matter which side of the attacker they are on.

The team in possession of the ball is the attacking team; the team without the ball is the defending team. There are no half measures, and it doesn't matter what number is on your shirt.

The aim of the defending side is to win the ball. As we have seen, this can be achieved by tackling. However, attackers are becoming increasingly wily and clever at shielding the ball; and referees are becoming increasingly quick to clamp down on the slightest mistimed challenge. For these reasons, many teams simply opt to make life as difficult as possible for the attacking side. Instead of tackling, the defending team concentrates on getting players goal-side, then putting pressure on the man in possession. By closing him down and denying him time and space, the defending side exerts a lot of pressure. The player on the ball might be forced into a negative pass, a risky forward pass or a dribble. If he opts to pass, it could be

misdirected - offering the possibility of an interception. Alternatively if the receiver is also immediately put under pressure, he might miscontrol the ball.

If the attacker chooses to dribble, the defender should not commit himself. Again, the tactic should be to jockey and harry, and, if possible, force your opponent towards the touchline or square across the pitch.

Note that defending in this way requires good movement and positional play, with every outfield player helping to crank up the pressure on the attacking side. There is no technique involved until the defending side forces a mistake and manages to intercept or make a tackle.

Slide tackle

While running alongside your opponent, take off on the inner foot and swing the outer foot around your body as you fall. The outer foot should either hook itself around the ball or push it away.

GOALKEEPING

Peter Enckelman
in action

The goalkeeper is the single most important member of the team. Outfield players might have technical weaknesses, play badly or even "hide" on the pitch. After a game, few people remember such individual performances, especially if the game has been won. And even if they do remember a poor individual display by an outfield player, it can be hard to relate it to the final score.

These luxuries aren't open to the goalkeeper. There is nowhere to hide, and any blunders or flaws in his technique usually result in him picking the ball out of the back of his net.

On the positive side, goalkeepers can win games just as well as prolific strikers. Coaches often talk about a team needing a strong spine, and that starts with the goalkeeper. Coaches know that a top-class 'keeper can be worth 10 points per season to a side. The dividing line between success and failure is so narrow that a quality goalkeeper can make the crucial difference.

What makes a good goalkeeper?

Goalkeepers are usually tall; they certainly must be a dominant physical presence in order to command their box and instil confidence in the defence. 'Keepers need to be agile and athletic, with excellent reflexes and hand-eye coordination. And as far as physical attributes are concerned, let's not forget a good pair of hands!

Goalkeepers have to be brave, prepared to go for the ball when attackers' boots might be flying. They must be cool when they are under pressure, and able to maintain high levels of concentration when they're not. Finally, between the sticks is no place to be if you are a shrinking violet! Communication is vital, and in the heat of the game that usually means bawling at the top of your voice. Watch David James or Peter Schmeichel in action and you'll see how clearly they make their views known to

their team-mates! This is very important, as the 'keeper is often well placed to spot any danger signals and marshal his defence to deal with them.

Taking the ball palms down with eyes fixed on the ball.

SHOTSTOPPING

The range of shots that a 'keeper has to deal with is almost endless. They fire in at different heights and from different angles. One attacker might go for sheer power, another clever placement. The ball can dip or swerve. And if that's not enough, there are the extra uncertainties of being unsighted, bobbles off the turf and deflections off players. Nevertheless, there are some basic principles which 'keepers should heed when dealing with shots.

- **Be alert and on your toes** - quite literally. The ideal position is on an imaginary line between the ball and the centre of the goal-line. This line obviously changes as the ball travels across the field and the 'keeper should adjust his position accordingly.

- **Keep your eye on the ball.** If an attacker is shaping to shoot, don't be distracted by anything else that is going on.

- **Get as much of your body as possible** behind the ball. Ideally, take the ball with both hands, with the body behind as a secondary barrier. If there is time, move your body into position instead of diving.

- **Sideways steps.** If you do have time to move across your goal, use sideways steps; don't cross your legs.

- **Two hands are better than one.** If you can't get your body behind the ball, two hands are better than one. Spread the fingers of both hands behind the ball and bring it into the body as soon as possible.

- **Catch if you can,** punch if you are in any doubt. If you do opt to punch, go for height and distance, and put the ball out on to the flanks rather than down the middle of the pitch. For a shot dipping under the bar or just inside the post, a one-handed deflection is often needed. Use the palms of the hands to guide the ball over the bar or round the post. Conceding a corner is better than conceding a goal.

Ideally the goalkeeper should take the ball with both hands, with his body behind as a secondary barrier. If there is time, move your body into position instead of diving. The knees should be bent and legs apart to achieve a good base for balance.

When diving, push off on the leg nearest the ball

Maintain a sideways position through the air. It is easy to twist into a face-down position, and if that happens you won't be able to watch the ball.

When making a save, relax the part of the body that meets the ball

This will have a cushioning effect and make the possibility of a rebound less likely.

Sometimes goalkeepers need a bit of good luck

They may dive the wrong way and make a save with a trailing leg. It doesn't look pretty but it's just as effective as an elegant, swan-like dive. These kind of saves are often not as fortunate as they appear. The 'keeper is usually making himself as big a target as possible, increasing the chances of the ball hitting him. In any case, goalkeepers have such a hard job that they deserve the odd stroke of good fortune.

Peter Enckelman clasps the ball to his chest. Many 'keepers take the ball in the stomach area by diving towards it with the arms folded in behind to secure it.

One-on-one situations

We have already looked at how a goalkeeper should move across his goal, depending on the position of the ball. If an attacker is through on goal, he must also be ready to move forward. Coming out to meet the attacker will give the latter a much smaller target to aim at. This is known as narrowing the angle.

Advancing from the goal-line does bring dangers, however. If the 'keeper goes too far or not far enough, too early or too late, the attacker will have the upper hand. Depending on the 'keeper's position, the striker could shoot low, go for a chip, dribble or pass to a team-mate. The 'keeper should advance when the ball is beyond the attacker's playing distance. When the attacker has the ball under control, the 'keeper should check his run and take up a ready position.

Stay on your feet

Try to force the attacker wide, on to his weaker foot, or both. Don't go to ground too early; make yourself look as big as possible, perhaps with arms flailing to try to put the attacker off. When you do decide to go for the ball, wait for a moment when the attacker is looking at the ball or when it is beyond his playing distance. Spread yourself wide as you go down. If you don't manage to get the ball, you might have forced the attacker into a more difficult position from which to score, and perhaps gained time for your defenders to recover.

Diving

When diving, push off on the leg nearest the ball. Always try to maintain a sideways position through the air. It is easy to twist into a face-down position, and if that happens you won't be able to watch the ball. Take the ball with the palms down.

Fabien Barthez makes a save low to his right. He collapses the leg nearest to the ball and takes the ball with the palms down.

Always try and get two hands to the ball even when diving at full length.

DEALING WITH CROSSES

Relatively few attacks come straight through the middle, where the defence is strongest. More often, a team will attack down the flanks and put the ball into the box from wide positions. Dealing with these crosses is a key skill for a goalkeeper.

Taking up a good starting position is important. If the attacker is out wide, the 'keeper should be in the centre of the goal or slightly nearer the far post. It is easier to go forward than to back-pedal. If the attacker cuts in, the 'keeper should move towards the near post. For angled crosses from further out, the keeper should maintain a central position but advance to the 6-yard line.

When the ball is in flight, the goalkeeper must decide whether to go for it or not. The decision will be based mainly on the pace and trajectory of the ball, but the number of bodies that are in the way will also be a factor. Once his mind is made up, the 'keeper should be decisive. He should attack the ball at speed. A one-footed take-off will help to give maximum height, and the 'keeper should take the ball at the highest possible point.

Decide whether you are going to catch or punch early on, and stick to it. Punching will be safer in a crowded area or if you are back-pedalling. If you're not 100% confident of catching the ball, opt to punch. Try to gain maximum height and distance, and put the ball on to the flanks by preference.

Real Madrid goalkeeper Iker Casillas claims the ball at its highest point while under pressure from teammate Aitor Karanka and Barcelona's Rivaldo.

The goalkeeper as sweeper and attacker

The best 'keepers think and act like sweepers. They are always alert to balls played into space behind the defence. If the 'keeper can get to the ball first, he might be saving himself from a dangerous one-on-one situation.

The 'keeper's role in launching attacks is also important these days. Once he has the ball in his hands, quick, accurate distribution - either from a throw or kick - can be very effective in setting up counter-attacks.

Ball on the ground

This is the hardest save to make - that's why strikers keep the ball low. How you make the save will depend on how close the ball is to your body. If the ball is coming close to you, fall on to the ball. If it is slightly further away, collapse the nearest leg. The priority is to get the hands to the ground to meet the ball as quickly as possible. The body can follow on.

- Once your mind is made up, be decisive.

- Attack the ball at speed.

- A one-footed take-off will help to give maximum height.

- Take the ball at the highest possible point.

- Decide whether you are going to catch or punch early on, and stick to it.

- Punching will be safer in a crowded area or if you are back-pedalling.

- If you're not 100% confident of catching ball, opt to punch.

- Try to gain maximum height and distance, and put the ball on to the flanks by preference.

Tipping the ball over the bar

If the ball is too high to catch or too risky to punch, then tip it over the bar. Stretch as far as you can with one hand to give greater height and use an open palm to deflect the ball over the bar.

DEVELOPING SKILLS

Italy's Marco
Delvecchio on the
training ground.

The basic skill of balancing the ball on your foot will give a feeling of confidence and make you increasingly comfortable with the ball.

Practice usually comes with a clear purpose. We have looked at all the key footballing skills, with the purpose of making you a better player and increasing your all-round knowledge of the game. But there are some skills that you are unlikely to be able to use during a match.

Trying to master a trick will improve your overall feel for the ball. Moving the ball as shown in this sequence from the forehead to the back of the neck is one of the more advanced skills.

Basic juggling skills:

- Juggling the ball
- Trying to hold the ball on the instep or back of the neck
- Running towards a stationary ball and trying to flick it up and over your head

Tricks such as these are all good fun. Indeed, before and after practice sessions, all players love to have a go at their favourite party pieces. Do they matter? Should you bother with them? Yes, most definitely! Trying to master a trick or two is valuable for two reasons. First, it gives you the chance to express yourself and have some fun before the serious practice gets under way, or after it has finished. Second, it will improve your overall feel for the ball. There is an old footballing adage which says you should "make friends with the ball". What better way to build up a close friendship than to play around with it in this way? You may not be able to use these exact tricks in a game situation, but they will improve your overall touch and control - and you'll certainly need those skills.

The way in which the outfield players line up is a key element in a team's overall tactical approach to the game. Naturally, coaches have experimented with various formations and systems in an effort to improve performances and results. Neither a particular formation nor a precise set of tactics can guarantee success. What they can do is to help maximise the potential of the individual players.

Tactical decisions can give a team a vital edge, as the margin between success and failure is often extremely small. A good system uses the individual strengths of the players to the full. If there are any obvious weaknesses in the team, a formation should be adopted which makes it difficult for the opposition to exploit them.

DEFENSIVE FORMATIONS

Defensively, the main considerations are how many players to use, and whether or not to deploy a sweeper. For many years, four defenders were considered the norm. These days, many attacking sides might play with just one or two strikers. Having spare defenders is all very well, but it means a team must be outnumbered elsewhere. This is one of the factors behind the introduction of wing-backs in a 3-5-2 system in recent years.

It was the defence-minded Italians of the 1960s who developed the idea of playing a sweeper or "libero" (free player) behind the marking defenders. His job is to cover across the whole back line, and he must also co-ordinate the offside trap. Although the use of a sweeper was originally conceived as an ultra-defensive tactic, teams gradually became aware of the attacking potential of the libero. In particular, the great Dutch and German sides of the 1970s recognised that the sweeper was in a prime position to break forward and launch attacks. Remember, a team should not simply decide it wants to operate a sweeper system; instead, the coach must look at his available players and decide whether anyone has the skills required for this highly specialised role.

MIDFIELD FORMATIONS

The midfield area is universally acknowledged as the most important battleground on the pitch. The team that controls the midfield controls the match. This fact has informed every coach's thinking concerning formations in the modern era. At one time, the 4-2-4 system was very common, with two playmakers linking the defence and attack. This gradually gave way to 4-3-3 and 4-4-2. Today, some teams operate a 4-5-1 system, particularly for away games. You can see from this pattern that there has been a tendency to pack the midfield by pulling strikers into deeper positions. The recent trend to play with wing-backs in a 3-5-2 formation has had a similar effect, but this time by pushing defenders forward.

Strength in midfield

Certainly no team can afford to be overrun in midfield. However, if four or even five players are operating in this area, it is vital that they drop deep to bolster the defence, and break forward to support the attack. Of course, midfielders shouldn't all go forward or fall back at the same time. Good players watch how the play is developing and cover for each other as required.

Five forwards

Gone are the days when teams regularly lined up with five forwards. The 2-3-5 formation was very vulnerable defensively.

◄

Sweeper system

The great Dutch and German sides of the 1970s recognised that the sweeper was in a prime position to break forward and launch attacks. The Dutch philosophy of "total football" was based on the talents of Johan Cruyff. Ajax of Amsterdam won the European Cup with the 1-3-3-3 formation. ►

Gone are the days when teams regularly lined up with five forwards. Nowadays, the striker's role can be a very lonely one, particularly away from home. Most teams tend to play with two up front, sometimes only one. If other players join the attack, however, it can be devastating. Manchester United's success over the past decade has been founded on a basic 4-4-2 formation. The pace and fluid movement in the team have always meant that midfield players and defenders are quick to get forward when United are on the attack. If this kind of support is lacking, strikers - or the lone striker - can find themselves isolated and outnumbered.

Hunting in pairs

There is an old saying that strikers hunt in pairs. This can be a straightforward twin-pronged attack, or the more recent innovation of a split-striker set-up. In the latter system, one striker plays in a slightly withdrawn role. By dropping a little deeper, players in this position can sometimes find space more easily and make themselves difficult to mark. Teddy Sheringham and Paul Scholes are often used in this role to very good effect.

4-4-2

Manchester United's success over the past decade has been founded on a basic 4-4-2 formation with midfield players quick to get forward to join the attack.

Acknowledgements

Thanks to
Jane Hill, Richard Betts, Peter Wright,
Trevor Bunting, Simon Taylor,
Judy Spindler, Kelly Cantlon,
John Dunne, Oliver Clarke,
Daniel Groves, Jack Hylands,
Kilara Kilama-Oceng, Ubaid Nawaz, Richard
Trafford, Corinne Hill
and Jen Little